What This Book Will Do for You

By the end of this book, you will be able to use a variety of methods for improving your ability to remember names, words, speeches, phone numbers, faces, things you read and hear, and your important appointments. So read on . . .

Other Titles in the Successful Office Skills Series

Get Organized! How to Control Your Life Through Self-Management

How to Be a Successful Manager

How to Negotiate a Raise or Promotion

How to Read Financial Statements

How to Write Easily and Effectively

Increasing Your MEMORY POWER

Donald H. Weiss

amacom

American Management Association

This book is available at a special
discount when ordered in bulk quantities
For information, contact Special Sales Department,
AMACOM, a division of American Management Association,
135 West 50th Street, New York, NY 10020.

Library of Congress Cataloging-in-Publication Data

Weiss, Donald H., 1936-
    Increasing your memory power.

    (The Successful office skills series)
    Includes index.
    1. Memory. 2. Mnemonics. I. Title. II. Series.
BF371.W42   1986   153.1'2   85-26885
ISBN 0-8144-7645-7

Printing number

10 9 8 7 6 5 4 3 2 1

CONTENTS

Introduction—Putting Your Memory to Work   1

1. The Keys to Memory Improvement   3

2. Remembering Names, Faces, and Objects   18

3. Improving Your Word Power and Recall   22

4. Remembering What You Read   25

5. Remembering What You Hear   33

6. Remembering Your Own Speeches and Presentations   41

7. Remembering Numbers and Appointments   48

Conclusion   53

Index   56

About the Author   58

Introduction—
Putting Your Memory to Work

Life's embarrassing moments. Everyone's had them. Names forgotten, anniversaries overlooked, life's little incidents lost in the mists of time. This ever happen to you?

You: So you see, Mr. Jones, our product will replace the equipment you're now using at a greatly reduced cost.

Customer: [*Annoyed*] I suppose so, but the name's Smith, not Jones.

Or how about this?

You: I know I put my glasses down somewhere. I had them on while I was reading my book. [*With increasing agitation*] Now, where did I put them when I got up to get that glass of iced tea? I just *know* they're here. If I don't find those darned glasses, I'll—Oooh! I'm getting so mad!

Spouse: You mean those funny-looking eyes peering out of the top of your head?

Now, quick. What's your aunt's phone number? It's on the tip of your tongue, isn't it? Where is the letter you have to find for your boss? The presentation you have to make to the board tonight—are you ready to make it? If only you had room in your brain to store all that stuff.

The point is, *you do*. You do have room in your brain to store all that stuff and a whole lot more. In fact, the brain stores almost everything it experiences—whether or not you're aware of the experience itself. No computer yet invented can store the millions of pages of copy the brain theoretically could print out.

Your memory's not the problem. As a storehouse of information, nothing can beat it. Each nerve ending in the brain—and there are millions of them—stores a bit of information that positively charged ions send flying along from one nerve cell to another. That's happening all the time, without your being aware of it.

Storing information's no trick. Retrieving it—that's the rub. All that stuff's just sitting there, tucked away in synaptic knobs, waiting, languishing, while you scurry about wishing you had a better memory. And all the time it's just that you're not letting your memory do for you the work it's capable of doing.

When it comes right down to it, this is another fitness book—a muscle-building program. Well, the brain's not really a muscle, but as in the case of the muscles, it needs exercise, too. In fact, the analogy holds true for most people, insofar as they use far fewer muscles than they have, and scientists tell us we use no more than 20 percent of our brain power as well.

But you knew that. That's why you bought this book in the first place. You want to use a lot more of that brain power locked up in your head.

Well, I won't disappoint you. I intend to supply you with a fitness program for exercising your brain, by showing you ways to use your brain more effectively.

Chapter 1

The Keys to Memory Improvement

I can't make you want to improve your memory. You have to supply the "want to." The harder you work at improving your memory, the better and stronger your memory will be. Still, you need a method for taking advantage of your desire to improve your memory, and the method is essentially the same as you'd use for carrying out any exercise program: setting goals and working toward achieving them.

What reason do you have for wanting to improve the use of your memory? Give the question some serious attention.

Some people want their memories to work for them in order to improve their position at work. It's no secret that a person who can remember small details, who can recall important data, who can deliver a dynamic and intelligent presentation without notes—come promotion time, that person has a leg up on others. He or she is remembered.

Maybe you're like other people who just get darned tired of not being able to remember clients' names. Or of not being able to recall their sweetheart's phone number, let alone their great-aunt's. Remember, the role of attitude in learning (and in using what you learn) differs very little from the role of attitude in sports: You have to want to be a winner to win.

Enhancing Your Memory
Through Motivation

The "want to" has an important function in memory. Memory can either be a passive process over which you have no control or an active process that you can make work for you.

The storing of information—that's the key to understanding what memory is and how to increase its power. *The most important function of memory is to store information and images. The power of memory is the process of reviving or reliving experiences.*

To begin to improve your memory, you have to want to pay closer attention to the world around you, to the things that are happening to you and to other people. You have to want to pay closer attention to what you read or hear in order to store that information as *readily accessible memories,* as opposed to *inaccessible memories.*

Now, I've already said that the brain stores far more of your experiences than you realize or ever have need to revive or relive deliberately. Some of that storehouse of information lies close to the surface of consciousness; that's the meaning of readily accessible memories. Most of it lies buried, out of the way until needed. And some of it lies buried away never to be retrieved or to be retrieved only with great difficulty; this is the meaning of inaccessible memories.

Though it seems odd to talk about "inaccessible memories," I do so because *one critical way of improving your memory is to prevent experiences from being stored inaccessibly—to work at keeping your important experiences in accessible memory.*

Most people pay little attention to the ordinary events in their lives. Yet those experiences register in their brains whether or not they observe them. Many such experiences wind up in the never-never land of inaccessible memory, waiting to be dredged up either by expert manipulation or through some traumatic experience that somehow or other rings the bell of familiarity.

In addition, everyone stores experiences or information he or she would sooner not remember—office gossip, a serious error he or she made in a report or other important document, painful experiences, bad news, rumors. Some of those pieces of information people deliberately forget. Psychologists call it "suppression."

People also store other bits of information without ever really being aware of them in the first place. Then, when they need that information, it's missing. They get into arguments or fail to correct problems that stem from the events they've lost mentally.

The first step in increasing the power of your memory is to control the amount and types of information you suppress or allow to pass unnoticed and, as a result, store inaccessibly.

When something happens that you don't like or that hurts you, you could suppress it, or you could deal with it openly at the time it happens, acknowledging the hurt, accepting it, and doing what you have to do to make it hurt less. Working to live with the experience keeps you from pushing it so far down in your mind that you can't retrieve it on your own. It keeps the memory fairly alive and easy to recall. When the experience is no longer an immediate issue, you place it into that zone called the threshold of consciousness—or simply, accessible memory.

Most important memories hang suspended in accessible memory, fairly readily available for easy recall or recollection. That's the place to which you want to send as many of your experiences or as much of the information you gather as you can. Whether the experiences or information are painful or joyful, or emotionally neutral, only by controlling how you store the memories of your immediate affairs can you be sure you won't forget important events.

At the same time, just imagine what a buzzin', bloomin' confusion your life would be if you remembered *all* your experiences *all* of the time. Your attitudes and values, tastes and interests help the brain decide *where* and *how* to store its data—deep (at relatively inaccessible levels) or close by (at the *threshold of consciousness*), readily accessible for use when needed—by determining what you store as *meaningful memory.*

You remember things, events, people, and so on that are important to you, that have value or are of interest to you. They are your meaningful memories.

Your attitudes and values, tastes and interests also affect meaningful memory by determining how much of your memory you use at any given time. What seems important or interesting to you at the time, you remember readily. What seems unimportant or uninteresting at the time, you push from your consciousness.

People almost always automatically pay more attention to something of interest to them, to what they care about, or to what's important to them. Conversely, their casual experiences that seem uninteresting or unimportant—at the moment—they let pass with little *immediate recognition.*

But here's where you can take charge. Use meaningful memory to separate experiences into those you want to place into accessible memory and those you want to place into inaccessible memory. Rather than let events dictate the process, you make the choices yourself whenever possible. You decide what is important to remember and what is not.

You can't decide in advance, it's true, just how important any and every experience is destined to be—someday. Still, you can make some reasoned judgments about what value an experience might have for you. Consider three ways of looking at an experience or at some bit of information or at some set of data.

First, you determine something's importance when you answer the questions "What would happen if I don't remember this? Would it make any difference to me and/or to other significant people in my life?" If it makes no difference whether you forget it, it's obviously not important.

On the other hand, though it might make a difference to you or to someone else if you remember something, it may not be as important as it seems when you consider a second issue. How immediately do you need to use that information or refer to that experience? The name of the client you're visiting this morning—that's pretty immediate. That report you have to deliver to the board in the morning, that's pretty immediate, too. So you need to ask, "When will I need this information? How soon or late?"

Finally, you guarantee something's urgency if other things depend on it—such as your promotion to vicepresident. Test the real importance of an experience by its degree of fruitfulness relative to subsequent events.

You might say, then, that the most important things to remember are those things that make a difference to you and/or to other people, are needed right away, and on which other things depend. Given those three criteria for *setting priorities,* you're now in a position to eliminate one of the most important barriers to a good memory: *clutter.*

You know what clutter is. It's the brain's version of jamming. It's the bloomin', buzzin' confusion of daily life. And it's the preoccupation with a given set of memories. The preoccupation with one set of memories—that's the clutter that produces *absentmindedness.*

Absentminded people usually focus their attention on things other than the situation at hand. Their forgetfulness is selective, the selectivity flowing from their own priorities. They forget—that is, they don't think about—things that aren't important, immediate, or fruitful for them. Their high-priority items occupy their conscious mental activities, or their most personal concerns or interests float close to the surface of their threshold of consciousness. Everything else becomes relatively inaccessible. They seem to forget things everyone else thinks are important. They seem not to have what everyone else thinks is common sense. They seem to require more reminders of one kind or another than most other people.

Though the brain automatically reduces the confusion of everyday experiences, to reduce the clutter even more and to prevent absentmindedness, you have to set priorities that separate out from among those experiences the ones you need to retrieve easily. Your priorities help pigeonhole experiences—classify them—for orderly filing. It's like putting labels on them.

1. That's *really important.*
2. This other thing seems *pretty important.*
3. That's *important*, too.
4. These things are *trivial* or *unimportant.*

Since your priorities depend on your attitudes and values, tastes and interests, your priorities also shape your meaningful memory. Your mental and emotional sets, how you feel about the world around you, and how you see it determine what to you seems important, seems immediately needed, and seems fundamental to other things. You have to take into consideration those *subjective* aspects of your life as well as the rational criteria you might use when setting priorities.

A large portion of meaningful memory is need-driven because most of human behavior is need-driven. A great deal of what people do has purpose or direction, as attempts to satisfy some need or another—such as learning skills in order to get a job or to advance in a current job.

When you're aware of your needs, you consciously set goals to meet them. Other times, you set goals without even realizing that you've done it— as when you're hungry, and you decide on a menu for satisfying the hunger. Goal-directed behavior and goal-directed information are remembered better than arbitrary behavior or random bits of information. Your interest in the activity or the information *fixes your attention* on it and holds it there.

It follows, therefore, just as in the case of athletes, that the more goal-directed you become, the more you'll remember what you've done or learned—that is, the more you'll enhance your memory. The more goal-directed you become in your relationships with people, the better you'll remember their names or other pertinent facts about them. The more goal-directed you become, the more successful you'll become at whatever you try to do.

The "want to" by itself, however, won't get you very far. You need to have a firm grasp on *what* you want to accomplish, *by when* you want to accomplish it, and *how* you'll get to that goal. Without goal setting, you could actually demotivate yourself by having nothing to guide you, to let you know how well you're doing, or to make you feel good about what you're doing.

Let's say that you want to improve your vocabulary.

The "Want To"

Without a desire to change, self-improvement becomes tedious and self-defeating. Any attempt to raise the power of your memory to the level of its potential has to begin with a "want to."

1. Decide on what you want to change and what needs the change will meet.
2. Set priorities among your targets and work only on those that have the greatest importance, immediacy, and fruitfulness.
3. Write goals and objectives for each program of change.
4. Develop a comprehensive action plan and work at your plan regularly and diligently.
5. Reward yourself every time you achieve an objective.

How many words a day do you want to retain and recall easily? How are you going to go about doing that? Answering what, when, and how helps you focus your interest.

For example, if you say you want to learn to use appropriately five new words a day, you know *what* you want to do. You know *when* you'll do it—every day (that could easily be for the rest of your life). Then, to help you sustain your interest as well as to give you guidance, answer *how*. That'll keep you looking for new sources—dictionaries, and encyclopedia, the *Reader's Digest*.

The goal also helps you sustain your interest, because when you know what you want to accomplish, accomplishing it feels good. Your success reinforces the learning.

Once you've set up your goals and objectives, you'll be well on your way to success. Still, without that initial desire—that "want to"—you might as well put this book back on the shelf and stumble on through life wondering where you misplaced your glasses.

Enhancing Your Memory Through Observation

Memory is the storehouse of information or images, or the process or reviving or reliving our experiences. No one knows just how the brain stores all our experiences. What is known is that you can improve your recall by keeping your experiences fresh and accessible. One sure way to improve your memory is to become more observant. You can then use other techniques—for example, visualization and association—for drawing upon experiences careful observation has captured in accessible memory.

Seeing, hearing, feeling, smelling, tasting—each of the five senses plays a role in careful observation. To enhance memory effectively through observation, it's important to bring as many of the senses to bear at the same time as possible. To paraphrase a saying attributed to Confucius:

> Tell me and I hear,
> Show me and I see,
> Allow me to do, and I remember.

(The original last line is, "Allow me to do, and I understand.")

In this context, the word *do* means "to use as many

11

senses as possible." It means to gather your experiences into your mind as completely as you can, multiplying the number of sensory cues you can draw on for recognizing the experience or the information when you need it.

You shouldn't underestimate the role of recognition in observation. It comes to bear both during the experience itself and during the subsequent memory process. *In fact, the more you recognize in your immediate experience, the more likely you'll retain that experience in your accessible memory.*

You've had the experience, I'm sure, of interviewing for a new job in an environment strange to you. For example, as the department's secretary leads you throught the data processing center, you pass many machines that you do not recognize (assuming you're not a computer operator). The secretary will remember seeing specific machines that you'll say you never noticed. Well, you probably saw them, but you couldn't recognize them and register the experience in your accessible memory. The secretary could. When someone points out the machines to you and tells you their names, you'll recall having seen them—and now you'll be able to recall them even if they're not there in front of you.

Here's another example you may find familiar. The office manager buys a new copier—a make and model you've never seen before (or think you haven't seen). All of the sudden you see that copier everywhere you go. It's as if everyone in town has bought the identical make and model—even in the same color.

You know down deep that the other copiers have always been there. It's only that, until now, you didn't notice them. Now that your office has one, you recognize them—they're just like the one your office manager bought.

So one way to exercise the power of your memory is

to pay more attention to your experiences and deal with those experiences that you might otherwise push into inaccessible memory. Learn the names of things. Exercise your brain. An active brain, just as an active body, keeps you from slipping into sluggish habits.

But becoming more observant is only one way of increasing your memory power. Using *mnemonic devices*—from the root word *mneme* or "enduring basis for memory"—is another way. The two most useful mnemonic devices are visualization and association.

Enhancing Your Memory Through Visualization

Hypnotists and stress-management counselors have made the idea of visualization popular. Creative imagery helps retention in at least two ways. It exercises your brain, and it helps make anything you hear or read immediately recognizable to you. They're your own images.

Recognition, I've said, is essential to recalling or remembering or recollecting. However, it's not always easy to recognize a list of numbers or a list of names or a catalog of places. Tying those things to images—even silly ones—helps you recall them.

Visualization has a basis in the process of memory itself—*memory afterimage*. Usually associated with blunders and other embarrassing moments, memory afterimage consists of a peculiarly vivid revival of an experience a brief moment after it happened. The afterimage burns the experience into your threshold of consciousness, and you experience it again and again.

The ability to summon up images from your brain has its origin in early childhood experiences, during which your lack of language (symbolic representation) forced you to recreate your experiences as images. Without imaging, you never would've learned anything.

As you grew older, however, you tended to image less and less—you became more and more dependent on symbolic representation for your thinking. Practicing visualizing helps the process of memory.

For example, after you read these next instructions, close your eyes and smell the aroma of the coffee in your cup. (If you don't happen to have a cup of coffee in front of you, sniff out something else.) Now, let fly your imagination.

Image that cup of brew. What color is the coffee? What shape is the cup? Get a good mental image of it. Go ahead, do this little exercise before reading on.

See, you can image or visualize. Everyone can. (If you're old enough to remember the heyday of radio, then you know how to visualize better than the generations that grew up with television.) It's just that most people don't do it as much once they learn how to represent things and experiences to themselves with words.

Visualization lends itself exceptionally well to the process of *recall*—the process or representing a past experience to yourself by evoking an image or repeating words or numbers previously learned. Imaging doesn't necessarily make all your recall perfect, but it does help to tie each attempt at recall to an individual experience or object or name or number—especially if you're trying to remember them in order or in a sequence.

Enhancing Your Memory Through Association

You'll probably improve your recall even more thoroughly by using the *principal of association,* the process of linking a vivid mental image with a fact, an experience, a name, a number, a face, or whatever.

Psychologists sometimes break association into six types: similarity, opposites, togetherness, frequency, recency, and vividness.

Anyone who has seen those psychological who-dunits at the movies is familiar with the *law of similarity.* It involves those free-association tests they give in which the doctor says a word and asks the patient to say the first word or phrase that pops into his or her head. Those associations are said to have specific meanings for the patient that indicate to the doctor from what types of disorders the poor wretch is suffering.

You can use the same principle as a mnemonic device. If two objects seem to be alike in some way, or at least complement each other, you link them together. Let's say you need to buy a can of coffee on your way home from work today. When first you realize you need to buy the coffee, fix two images in your mind: (1) a cup of steaming hot coffee, along with its aroma, and (2) the way you feel just before you drink that first cup of coffee in the morning.

Now, every time you see a cup of coffee today, think of how you'll feel if you don't drink that first cup of coffee tomorrow morning. Think of that first cup you wouldn't have if you don't remember to stop at the grocery store to pick up a can of coffee. Just before leaving the office, pick up your coffee cup and wash it out. The association of that cup with buying a can of coffee will come immediately to mind.

If two words or experiences have similar meanings, you can connect them together in some logical way, as in cause and effect. The recollection of one should remind you of the other. Even similar-sounding words can help jog your memory, whether or not they have anything in common. Sound-alikes—such as *jam* and *ham, hat* and *rat, pill* and *hill*—become habitually linked in the threshold of consciousness.

Opposites produce a similar linkage. That's why in those psychological whodunit movies, the patient frequently responded to the doctor's word with a word diametrically opposed to the first word's meaning. Why? In spite of characteristics unique to each person, anyone's brain tends to connect opposites together: *black* and *white, over* and *under, hot* and *cold, dark* and *light,* and so on. Like the law of similarity, the *law of opposites* appears to some psychologists as essentially an automatic reflex of the brain.

Not so the *law of togetherness.* This refers to learned behaviors. If you habitually use two ideas or impressions together, or otherwise experience them together regularly, you'll recall one by thinking of the other. What ideas or impressions you link together depends on where you grew up, how you were raised, how you were educated, and so on. The historical facts of your life condition the linkages you make.

Another principle of learned association I'll discuss later at length: the *law of frequency.* Repetition and spaced repetition, the recital or rehearsal of materials over and over, adds to your ability to recall anything learned—names, numbers, whatever.

Since old ideas fade, past experiences get shrouded in the mists, with new ideas or impressions replacing them fairly easily. The *law of recency* says that newer ideas or experiences are more readily retrieved than older ideas or experiences. That stands to reason, doesn't it?

To prevent new ideas and experiences from cluttering up the old ones or covering them over, spaced repetition helps keep the older material fresh in the mind. By recalling those ideas or events periodically, you not only remember them but you tend to keep them relatively accurate.

Finally, there is the *law of vividness.* We tend to

remember vivid impressions more accurately and for longer periods than dull ones. Anything that makes a strong impact on your senses will linger, as I pointed out in discussing memory afterimage. Larger-than-life images, caricatures, or anything ridiculous impacts on you, and that impact reinforces the experience or the idea or the fact.

When trying to learn a sequence of things or names, you can image something that you will always associate with the name or thing or whatever it is you're trying to learn. For example, if you're trying to remember a list of names of people coming to an important meeting, you can tie each name to some totally silly thing. Adams—a knobby Adam's apple bobbing up and down in a skinny throat. Brown—a parched, windblown landscape obscured by brown swirling dust.

Notice the action words? *Bobbing up and down, windblown, swirling.* Action makes imagery more vivid. That's why the TV beats out the printed word if you're trying to read in front of a turned-on set. Action catches your attention and rivets it to the image with which it's associated. Combine the vivid image and the action, and you have a strong device for remembering things.

You can use these fundamental laws and principles of learning and remembering to design interesting and fun ways to improve your memory. No one method is better than any other, because all of them are just different ways of applying the principle of association and combining it with the technique of visualization. In subsequent chapters, I'll apply those ideas to remembering names and faces, what you hear and read, phone numbers, and speeches or other presentations. I can show you how to use these ideas, but you'll have to supply the motivation to learn them and to put them into practice.

Chapter 2

Remembering Names, Faces, and Objects

Most of the time, remembering names or faces requires little more than some simple form of visualization or association. For example, you meet someone named Harry. What does the name sound like (the law of similarity)? Hairy. How much hair does Harry have? A lot—a heavy beard, long hair, hair on his hands? Again, the law of similarity. Harry is hairy. Now, visualize a hairy Harry, and, if you want, use the law of vividness. Make Harry as hairy as you wish.

What if he's not hairy? What if Harry's bald? Now, you can use the law of opposites. Harry's *not* hairy. If Harry's only partially bald, you may want to use the law of vividness to picture him with no hair at all.

Or if Harry's with a woman when you meet him, use the law of togetherness. Most women have relatively longer hair than a bald man. Think of Harry with the woman. If Harry's bald, you'll probably remember his name if you tell yourself, "Harry's the bald man with the hairy woman."

On the other hand, you may suffer from a problem many people have. They don't recognize people they've met before. Names seem to float in some disembodied form. "Oh, yes, I met Harry." But when they come face to face with Harry, they don't recognize him.

Once more, the power of observation, coupled with association and visualization, comes to the rescue. Notice the shape of Harry's face, the color of his eyes, the fullness of his lips. What do they remind you of? (Use the law of similarity.) Really study his face and tie the image to something with which you're already familiar—even if the connection seems funny (that is, obeys the law of vividness).

But if these simple connections don't seem to work for you, don't be dismayed. You're probably not paying attention in the first place. You have something else on your mind. You're thinking about what you want to say. You're trying to say something at the same time. Or plainly, you really don't care one way or another about remembering the names you hear or the faces you see. It's not a matter of memory. You can't forget what in all probability you haven't learned in the first place.

Changing that sort of so-called forgetfulness is really very easy. Here's where you can apply the full power of observation and handily visualize or put into practice an aspect of principle of association. In-depth observation has to come first. Combine as many sense experiences as you can.

Listen and use some form of association—let's say, the law of similarity—to nail down what you hear. The next time you meet a person for the first time, listen to the sound of the name. What does it sound like? A hard, clicking sound, such as *Teddy?* A soft, gentle sound, such as *Michele?* How does the sound fit the person?

To answer those questions, you have to listen. Repeat the name immediately. "Hello, Teddy." "You said 'Michele.' Is that right?" As you say it, you hear it again. Listen to your own voice saying it.

To decide if the sound fits the person, you have to look closely at him or her. Does he or she appear sturdy and strong, brittle or weak, soft or firm? Connect the visual impression with the sound.

At the same time, notice hair and eye coloring, skin

19

coloring. Dark or light? A color you can connect with Teddy or Michele or not? Tie together as many cues as you can.

And while you're looking at the person, listen also to the sound of the voice, not just to the sound of the name. See if the sound of the voice fits for you with the name and what he or she looks like. Add more cues.

And yes, touch and smell. Shake hands. Feel the texture of the skin. Feel the firmness (or lack of it) of the grip. At the same time, discreetly try to detect an aroma—a perfume or a cologne or an after-shave. Don't be embarrassed. The other person wouldn't wear it if he or she didn't want anyone to notice it.

Now you have a whole person with whom to associate the name. Teddy is that sturdy, blond man with the firm handshake, the gruff voice, and a strong scent of after-shave. He's not at all what you expect from a Teddy. Make up a complete and vivid description based on his name: Teddy Bear Gruff.

Michele is the short, dark-haired woman with the chubby hands and gentle voice—soft person with a soft-sounding name. How about Misty Michele?

All those cues taken together give you an experience you'll easily recognize any time you need to recall that person's name.

You can use the same power of observation to remember where you put things. Let's take the perpetual hunt for the mislaid glasses. Most people drop them down just anywhere, unheeding. They don't pay attention to what they're doing, even when they're not rushed or otherwise involved with something. It's a trivial thing, and they don't give it a second thought—until they need their glasses again.

You replace your thoughtlessness habit by experiencing putting down the glasses rather than just dropping them off somewhere. When you put down those glasses, look about you. See the surface on which you're placing them. Is it dark or light-colored? Is it pockmarked or even? Is it high up or low down or somewhere in between? Make a note of what the place looks like.

Now look at the glasses. Are they lying open on the rims and stems, or are the stems folded against the rims? Are they lying flat, lenses up, or flat, lenses down? Picture in your mind what the glasses look like, lying there on that surface.

Now touch the surface and the glasses. Is the surface hard or soft? Rough or smooth? Hollow or solid? Rub the surface. Tap it. Give yourself something to remember it by.

Touch the glasses, feeling the point of contact between the glasses and the surface. Fix that sensation in your mind.

Listen to the sound of the glasses touching that surface. Is it a light tap on a hard surface or a whishy sound on a soft surface? Hear the sound and think about what it reminds you of. Fix that connection in your mind.

Finally, use your sense of smell. (At least I'm not saying to taste the experience, too!) Especially if you're in the kitchen, sniff the air to sense any aroma that may be present. The last cue you give yourself may be the very one that triggers the recollection of where those darned glasses are.

You see what I'm telling you to do? Instead of dropping the glasses just anywhere, unheeding, give yourself the benefit of the full experience of putting them down.

That doesn't mean that you have to do *everything* that deliberately all the time. Yet as you work toward improving your memory, deliberate, conscious actions eventually become second nature, and what takes a minute or longer in the beginning will take no more than a split second later.

Remembering names, faces, and other things requires an act of will and a willingness to work at training your mind to make the necessary observations and associations. As with any exercise, practice makes each success a little easier to achieve.

Chapter 3

Improving Your Word Power and Recall

An active brain underlies your ability to recall or relive past experiences deliberately. Your memory, in this sense, consists of experiencing (including learning or memorizing), retaining your experience, recalling it, and recognizing it as one you had in the past.

I'm talking about getting more use out of your accessible memory, the information stored in the threshold of consciousness. I've talked about enriching that storehouse of memories by enriching your life through observation. Now, I'll talk about practical methods that keep your memories close at hand and help you tie together different experiences into meaningful patterns: developing your word power through enlarging your vocabulary.

Remember the example earlier of going for a job interview and passing through the machine room of a data processing center, not knowing one machine from another? You can build your vocabulary simply by asking people to identify each machine in the room. That's a sorter, this is a laser printer, and so on.

Another way to build your vocabulary of words that name specific things is to learn the words before you come into contact with the things. That takes memorization and recall, but learning words that refer to things prior to experiencing the items themselves makes the association between words and their referents quicker, easier, and more complete. You can hear the name of the thing or read it. You get a description of it and its functions. The words and their definitions are there in your accessible memory. All you need now is the opportunity to connect them with the things themselves.

Memorization and recall strengthen word power whether you learn words that refer to things or those that refer to concepts (so-called abstract words). Say you want to learn a list of new words. Most people use repetiton as an effective way to learn new bits of unconnected data. Merely repeating the new material over and over (rote memorization) will help you retain it. But you already knew that, didn't you?

What you probably don't know is that mere repetition produces only short-term memory. *You'll lose nearly all of that information within 24 hours unless you repeat the activity of memorizing the material within a short time after the first attempt.* You'll retain even more of it if you'll repeat the same exercise several times over an extended period.

When developing a more powerful vocabulary, it pays to set a goal of learning a few new words every day—say, four or five. In the beginning, decide to work on a vocabulary that is related to work. Remember what I said about needs. We retain and recall much more easily things for which we have some sort of need.

Find the words and their definitions in whatever sources you have available: a dictionary, a manual with a glossary, a textbook. Write down each word and its primary definition (if it has more than one use). Then write each word in a simple sentence, using the word in its primary sense. For example, take the word *contractor:*

One that contracts or is party to a contract: as **a:** *one that contracts to perform work or provide supplies on a large scale* **b:** *one that contracts to erect buildings.*

That definition comes from Webster's *Ninth New Collegiate Dictionary.* Now, use it in a sentence.

The contractor was on time with his delivery of the raw materials.

Use the word every chance you get. Not only repeat it and its definition by themselves, but use the word meaningfully as well.

What about words with more than one definition? *Contractor* is one such word.

After feeling confident that you've captured the primary definition, repeat your exercise with the secondary definition. In this case, the secondary definition—"something (as a muscle) that contracts or shortens"—has nothing to do with the primary definition.

To help remember that second meaning, you could use the principle of association: "A contractor gives our company muscle by shortening the time it takes to get the work done."

Memorizing words as I just showed you will help you build your memory, not only by adding to your vocabulary but also by adding to your powers of observation. You'll own more words to use to describe what you observe, and those words will help suspend your experiences in accessible memory.

Chapter 4

Remembering What You Read

Another way to build your vocabulary is through reading (reading properly, that is). Most people don't read well, and that's one important reason why they don't build their vocabularies through reading and why they don't remember much of what they read.

In this section, I'll show first how to build your vocabulary through reading and then how to read more effectively, which in turn will show you how to remember more of what you read.

Most people read superficially. They let their eyes skim over words they don't understand. They let the context of what they read carry the meaning of new words. The result is they don't really know the words they've read.

Reading with a dictionary at hand solves that problem. Whenever you read something, check out a new word in the dictionary and then do the exercise I've already described. You'll add power to your vocabulary and retain more of what you've read. It takes longer to read through a piece, that's true, but then, no exercise builds any muscle overnight.

Now, how about improving reading skills in general? The inability of many people to remember what they read stems from faulty reading habits rather than from poor memory. They read superficially, they read too slowly, and they reread too often. If you suffer from any or all of those poor reading habits, by correcting them, you'll improve your memory automatically.

People read superficially not only by skimming over words they don't know but also by letting too many things—especially television—distract them while they read. They often read with little or no real understanding, and in the competition for their brain's single-minded focus, the multidimensional, active visual and auditory impressions win out over the one-dimensional, static printed word.

An obvious solution to that problem, and a genuine aid to memory, is to turn off the television when reading. *The brain concentrates on only one thing at a time.* It can flash back and forth between two different things, but in so doing, it loses its ability to keep one or both of the experiences in the readily accessible threshold of consciousness. Therefore, you pay a severe price if you try to read or learn something in front of a TV or when listening to your favorite rock star or opera singer.

Many people also tend to read too slowly, losing the train of thought, forgetting what they've just read before they finish the page it's on. That's because they tend to vocalize as they read, either to themselves or out loud.

Subvocal speech slows reading speed to near speaking speed, and unless you're a very rapid speaker, that speed is pretty tedious. Speaking subvocally with attendant tongue or mouth movements slows the reader even more, and speaking out loud while reading slows him or her significantly. Pronunciation becomes more important than meaning. Without meaning, as I've pointed out before, retention becomes more difficult.

The solution: Practice reading without subvocalizing or vocalizing. You'll read more, you'll read faster, and you'll remember more of what you read.

Students of reading habits say that most people reread too much. They call it regression—rereading materials already read. Doing that tends not only to slow them down but also to interfere with their grasp of the material. If you find yourself regressing, you need to learn how to *review* instead. Reviewing helps retention.

When reading material with which you're familiar, and in which few new words appear, don't interrupt the flow of your reading. Absorb the text as you're reading it. Go back later to fill in gaps. That's what I mean by reviewing.

Whereas regression slows you down and interferes with comprehension and retention, reviewing aids comprehension and retention by fleshing out details and filling in gaps. As you read, without interrupting the flow of your reading, pick out the salient or essential elements for remembering. Make mental notes of them. (In the following section, I'll talk about making written notes.) When you've finished reading the material you want to recall, stop and try to recapture in your memory all those salient points. If you have difficulty recalling them, go back to the material to review.

Taken together, those three basic reading flaws drastically impede good retention of what we read. All three problems can be overcome and reading retention improved if you practice reading without vocalizing, practice reading without regression, and practice with review.

Reading for Acquaintance and Reading for In-Depth Understanding

To make remembering what you read easier for yourself, consider two different, but not mutually exclusive, types of reading: (1) reading for *acquaintance* and (2) reading for *in-depth understanding*. It's in the second type of reading that you can use the cue-word outline, which I'll explain in a minute.

Few people can read everything printed in their fields. Managers, engineers, physicians, attorneys—it doesn't matter. They're inundated with journals and books telling them what they need to know, what they should know, and a whole lot stuff that would be inconsequential for them to know.

Just as you have to set priorities for what you need to or should remember, you have to set some priorities for what you read. You need to be selective in order to prevent unnecessary clutter. When it comes to books and magazines, you can weed through the rubbish easily enough just by *scanning* the table of contents and turning to only those topics that seem important or relevant to your real needs. You'll use your *meaningful memory* more effectively that way.

Given the volume of written matter available, you'll make life easier and reduce the clutter in your brain by reading for acquaintance most of the stuff that comes across your desk or sits on your coffee table in the living room. Reading for acquaintance means *getting the gist of the subject matter without developing a thorough or deep understanding of it.* Scanning, previewing, and skimming are three techniques well suited for reading for acquaintance.

In scanning, you look only for relevant or pertinent materials—specific facts or ideas. You do that when you look at a table of contents in order to select a specific article or chapter to read. You do the same in the text itself, especially if you're looking for readily identifiable items—such as charts, tables, and statistical summaries. By leaving out all other extraneous material in the text, you focus your attention sharply and eliminate all forms of clutter. In effect, you are using the process of reviewing by picking the salient or essential elements covered by the author out of the text. Then, using spaced repetition, if you need to use that information, you fix it in your threshold of consciousness and call it up whenever you need it.

Previewing is a highly selective form of reading that gives you a chance to decide what to skim (which I'll discuss next) and what to read for in-depth understanding. Every well-written article or chapter of a book tells you what to read, insofar as every paragraph has a topic sentence or a summary sentence that tells you what the paragraph is about. There are headings and subheadings that tell what whole groups of paragraphs have to say. Before reading the entire article or chapter word for word, preview the material to get a feel for what is essential for you to know in depth and what you can easily skim.

When you skim a page, you move your eye rapidly down the page, taking in headings, subheadings, topic sentences, and cue words that supply more than just the salient ideas you picked up by previewing. The cue words deepen your comprehension, and you retain that information in your threshold of consciousness—again, without interference from all the other extraneous background information on the page. By the way, most people use skimming techniques when they say they speed-read.

All three methods of reading for acquaintance give you a superficial knowledge of the materials you read, while, at the same time, they help you dig out facts and other specific bits of information. Reading for in-depth understanding, on the other hand, empowers your memory to fill your conversation with all the essential ingredients of what you read—without memorization. Reading for meaning taps *meaningful memory* to its fullest extent.

Don't read anything word for word the first time you

go through its pages. Whenever you put your hands on any type of printed matter, scan, preview, and skim. That way you'll know for sure what you should read for in-depth understanding before you get underway and not get hung up on a lot of detail that may or may not be important.

Setting priorities for what you read only begins the process of increasing your recollection of what has been read. You get the greatest amount of gain by increasing your comprehension. That's why I make such an issue of improving your vocabulary as a way to improve your memory.

In addition to knowing more words to begin with, you improve your comprehension by taking a genuine interest in what you're reading. Real interest comes in the form of deciding in advance what objectives you hope to achieve through the reading, by paraphrasing, selecting, organizing, and evaluating what you read—and by using a cue-word outline.

A cue-word outline is an effective tool for use in reviewing. It consists of an organized list of topics covered by the author. It's called a cue-word outline because the list of topics literally cues your mind to recall the entire passage from which the cue word comes. The cue words contain the main concept or thrust of the passage, and that allows you to recall the whole of it.

During your first reading of something (reading for acquaintance), without interrupting the flow of your reading, you identify the salient or essential points. When you read for in-depth understanding you interrupt your flow and take notes—in the margin or on a notepad. You make a notation in your own words to fix the idea, the concept, or the instructions in your mind and then leave yourself with a written record to review should you have difficulty recalling the material.

This versatile tool can be used to remember what you hear and a speech you have to make as well as what you read. I'll have more to say about that in the following chapters.

In spite of the effectiveness of a cue-word outline for helping you review what you're trying to remember, nothing substitutes for paying close attention to what you're reading. Without a genuine interest in what's before your eyes, you defeat your whole purpose. You won't retain a tenth of what you read. The power of observation applies here, and remember what I said about possible distractions.

Goal setting gives you the most important guideline for all good reading habits. The purpose for reading this material tells you what you have to retain. The goal or objective directs your previewing, skimming, and scanning, and it focuses your attention on what you have to read for in-depth understanding.

Before sitting down to read, decide on why you're reading whatever it is. The goal and objectives identify the most meaningful material to store in your threshold of consciousness.

By paraphrasing, you put the author's ideas into your own words. They mean more to you that way. They're his or her ideas, but they're your words. Many people write notes (produce a cue-word outline) in the margin that restate a paragraph's topic or summary sentence. They, in effect, become subheadings. Textbook publishers leave room for that, and some of them actually write the notes for you. Use their notes for previewing or skimming, but ignore them when reading for in-depth understanding. *You need to put the notes in your own words.*

While penciling marginal notes helps with comprehension and retention, it can't compare with writing notes on a separate piece of paper as you read. Using this cue-word outline, you select the materials most important for you to remember. When you select those materials, you then organize them into the format in which you need them, and you can linger over them to evaluate and digest them. The cue-word outline gives you a tool for condensing the work into a whole that's meaningful for you.

A Cue-Word Outline of a Passage of Text

These cue words come from a sequence of paragraphs in the text you are reading. See if you can tie them back to their sources.

Genuine interest = close attention

Goal setting - guidelines - purpose

Paraphrasing - my own words

Organize - analyze - select

You can see how jotting down a word or two in the margin or on a notepad will help the reviewing process. When you write your cue-word outline, you read it after you've finished reading the article or chapter. Pick out the salient or essential elements for remembering. If your notes are extraordinarily thorough, you'll need little else for fixing the ideas in your threshold of consciousness, because the cue words will trigger the entirety of the material.

Sometimes, however, your notes themselves may appear cloudy or opaque. Then you review specific pieces of the writing with a specific intent. You fix that information more securely and completely. You almost nail it into place.

Reading for acquaintance and reading for in-depth understanding do not conflict with each other. The one actually enhances the other by reducing clutter and focusing your memory on those things that are most meaningful to you.

Chapter 5

Remembering What You Hear

You *forget* names because you don't listen to people when they tell you their names, right?

Well, most people forget a whole bunch of stuff because they're hearing but they're not really listening. They let too many things get in the way. They let their minds wander while other people are speaking. They don't really understand what's being said, but they don't stop the flow of words to ask questions for clarification. Other times, they think they understand, but they really don't, and consequently, the words don't really settle into meaningful memories. Sometimes, they let emotions get in the way of listening, and what they hear isn't what was said. They remember the events erroneously or misted over by a cloud of feelings. In short, they can't remember what they never really heard in the first place.

Consciously and deliberately following some simple guidelines for what I call *participative listening* will help you absorb more of what you hear, understand it better, and remember it more efficiently.

I use the name participative listening *to highlight the*

fact that effective listeners remember more of what other people say because they join with them in their conversation, becoming fully engaged in what the other person is saying.

Many people listen passively, letting unclear ideas slide by or letting confusion over facts remain unresolved. Others listen with half an ear, actively listening to their own thoughts while other people are talking. Participative listeners, on the other hand, enter into the conversation as a partner.

Here's another application of the power of observation. To participate in what the other person is saying, you first have to *pay full attention* to what he or she is saying. That means to clear all the decks—the physical one around you and the one inside your head. If you're in your office, put aside anything on which you've been working. Clear your desk, put things into file folders and close them, or put them into drawers. Don't let anything distract you. If you can't accept the interruption at that moment, arrange a time when you can set everything else aside.

Clearing your brain isn't as easy to do, but you can do it by remembering that your brain can't concentrate on two things at once. So really concentrate on what the other person is saying.

You listen much more rapidly than the other person speaks—almost six times as fast—and your mind wanders when you're listening to someone else talk. Your brain has too much time for filtering in your own concerns—that back-and-forth action I mentioned earlier that makes it seem as if you can concentrate on two things at once. Eventually, your own concerns, since they have more meaning and importance for you than the other person's, dominate. You hear the other person's words without really letting them seep into meaningful as well as accessible memory.

Though everyone would like to agree with Aristotle, that the human being is a rational animal, most people think emotionally. Most people hear what they want to hear, or put another way—*most people remember what they thought they heard.* Emotions or feelings or values or biases clutter their minds and act as filters that distort the interpretation of what was said.

Put yourself into this scene. You send a report upstairs to the vice-president of operations, and he or she says, "That section on the equipment in shipping doesn't make sense to me." You hear, "Your report on the equipment in shipping doesn't make sense." A subtle difference, but an important one.

You either blow up and challenge him or her ("What do you mean my report doesn't make any sense?"), or you feel bad about it ("I'm sorry. I'll rewrite it.")—when all the vice-president is saying is that he or she didn't understand one particular section.

Your emotions got in the way of your understanding. By distorting what you hear, *emotions distort what you remember.* Sometimes you remember *only the emotion*—and can't even remember what triggered it. When this type of emotional listening clouds your memory, it causes totally unnecessary problems for you and everyone else.

You can control the negative impact of emotions on your memory, and you can use positive emotions for enhancing it. First, let's control the negative impact of emotions.

Paraphrasing, a way of giving the other person *feedback,* controls emotional listening and avoids the barriers to effective memory that emotional listening creates. First, to give that kind of feedback, you have to suspend your feelings and restate what you think the other person said—as in the scene with the VP and the report on the shipping-room equipment.

You paraphrase what he or she said: "If I understood you, you think my report is confusing."

The VP responds with: "No. That's not it. I don't understand the technical data, that's all. I'd like you to explain it to me."

You'll now remember what the VP actually meant, not the distorted interpretation or your bad feelings. If you do remember them, you'll recollect them in their proper perspective: "I really felt a little foolish. I thought you meant that my report was badly written, and I got angry for a moment."

Paraphrasing serves another function, also. By paraphrasing, you summarize what the person is saying. That way, if your feedback is correct, you bring that part of the conversation to a close with the question, "Right?" and the answer, "Yes."

Those words signal your brain to store the information *in the form in which you put it.* It's fixed in the threshold of consciousness as *your* thought, even though it's the other person's information. In effect, you make the information yours, too. It becomes a piece of your meaningful memories.

Though the law of vividness has its roots in life's more embarrassing moments, you can use good feelings and positive emotions to enhance your memory, as well. Many people recall the fine details of events if they tie the experiences to their own good feelings about them. They suppress the details of painful experiences but hang on to the details of the good experiences. The more fun you build into your life, the better your memory will be. Use the law of vividness to associate experiences with funny things.

Another way to enhance your memory of what people say is to use your power of observation, by *making eye contact.* It helps your concentration, and it helps you identify nonverbal cues that you can tie to the verbal message you hear. By using more than one sense at a time, you enhance your listening and retain more of the experience more completely and accurately. You can then use visualization to help you remember what was said, and you can associate the words with facial expressions or other gestures.

Often people don't remember what they've heard because they really didn't understand what the other person said. *Asking questions for clarification* penetrates the barrier of confusion created by not understanding. Since few people have the courage to say, "I don't understand what you're saying," a simple question can get at the real meaning of what the person said while helping you save face at the same time. "To be sure I understand, are you saying such and such?"

If you're correct in what you understand, you'll store it in meaningful memory. if you're wrong, you'll store the corrected version of what the other person said.

The kinds of questions you use when asking for clarification make an important difference in what you remember. When you ask, "Do you mean that the totals in the fiscal report are wrong?" the other person can answer yes or no. That may be all that's required. You asked a specific question to get a specific answer. That is called a *closed-ended question.* Here you lay claim in your memory to a fact or an opinion or an expression of a feeling.

On the other hand, questions that begin with *what, why, who, when, where,* or *how* request elaboration, detail, explanation. They force the other person to respond to you with more than a simple yes or no. You have the opportunity here to increase your comprehension and thereby improve your memory of what was said.

Finally, you ensure that you will remember more of what you heard and remember it more accurately if, when the conversation is drawing to a close, you *achieve consensus.* That's a fancy way of saying that you and the other person agree that you understand each other. Unfortunately, most people end their conversations without ever trying to achieve consensus, or if they do try, they usually ask, "Do you understand?"

You know what happens if you assume the other person understands you. The word *assume* makes an ass of you and me *(ass - u - me).* If you assume you heard correctly or understand what the other person said, you run the risk of storing incorrect information. So close off the conversation by giving him or her feedback and getting your memory straight.

- -

Guidelines for Participative Listening

1. Give your full attention to the other person, clearing both the space around you and the space between your ears.
2. Make eye contact, storing visual as well as auditory cues.
3. Ask for clarification, using both closed-ended and open-ended questions appropriately.
4. Give informational feedback, paraphrasing what the other person said and asking for correction, if needed.
5. Achieve consensus—get agreement on what you believe was said or done in order to assure that what you remember actually happened the way you recollect it.

- -

By participative listening, you get the whole picture of what the other person is saying, and you comprehend it in the fullest sense of the word *comprehend,* which also means "grasped" or "stored in one's mind." Participative listening increases comprehension. Complete comprehension then enhances memory.

Improving Your Memory of Other People's Speeches

There are situations in which you can't use participative listening skills: when listening to other people's speeches. The cue-word outline that improves the memory of what you read helps here, too.

Remember what I said about the brain's ability to concentrate on two things at the same time? (Namely, it can't.) Therefore, extensive note taking, unless you take shorthand expertly, actually interferes with your ability to absorb what a speaker is saying.

On the other hand, remember I said that the brain takes in everything, even if you're not aware of it happening. Therefore, when listening to a speech, listen attentively to what the speaker is saying, jotting down the words he or she *emphasizes.* The speaker emphasizes those words because he or she *wants you to remember them.* They convey the essence of his or her message. Those words form your outline.

Then, when the speech is over, review the notes immediately. Fill in the gaps as you review those notes, and you'll be amazed at how much you've actually retained.

The cue words tie into complete ideas through association. Each cue refers to a specific thought in the speech. Each word becomes the basis for putting together the entire outline of the speech.

Here's another way to increase your word power. Earlier I talked about increasing your vocabulary (enlarging the number of words you can recall meaningfully) by improving your reading skill or by memorization and usage. Now you can apply the cue-word outline from listening to a speech (or from listening to something on the radio or television) as a tool for increasing your word power.

Frequently speakers use words with which people are unfamiliar. Usually the listeners let that slide by, drawing the meaning of the strange sounds from the context of what is said—just as they do when they read improperly. In short, they listen as superficially as they read. They don't learn anything new in the process, and moreover, that practice is fraught with danger.

A story circulates around the training and development profession that points out just how dangerous superficial listening can be. Whether or not the story is true, no one seems to know, but it has too strong a moral to overlook.

Some years ago, the story begins, a chapter of the American Medical Association and a group of psychologists set out to demonstrate that people don't really listen to what they hear, especially during one of those interminably long professional conferences. To make their point, they hired an actor to deliver a paper filled with jingoistic but impressive-sounding gibberish and to deliver the talk with great expressiveness and authority. In short, strongly worded double-talk. At the conclusion of the conference, the participants were asked to rate the presentations on the basis of interest as well as content and usefulness—and of all the talks, the actor's presentation received the highest ratings in both dimensions.

The moral? *For a large number of people, it's not what is said but how it's said that matters.* Even though the participants didn't really understand a word of what the actor said (and remembered even less of it), they thought they did. Had anyone been making a cue-word outline and looking up the words in his or her own reference sources, that astute listener would have realized that the audience had been had.

As I said, the story may be apocryphal, but it does show that you can make more sense of what you hear and remember more of it by using a cue-word outline to enhance the value of listening to a speech. Use it to check out the truth or validity of what the person is saying and (to meet your immediate objective) to increase your own word power by looking up the unfamiliar words the speaker used but didn't define. As you learn new words, you increase the accuracy as well as the detail in your memory of the speech. The cue-word outline and the fleshed-out definitions become powerful tools for reviewing what you've heard.

It follows, then, that if a cue-word outline will help you remember someone else's speech, it should help you remember your own speech, as well. And that's our next topic.

Chapter 6

Remembering Your Own Speeches and Presentations

Suppose you have to deliver a speech. If you're like other people, you'll find it easier to memorize a speech than a list of independent words, because the speech constitutes a part of what is called *meaningful memory*. Those are materials in which you have an interest, that have importance, that have immediacy, and on which other things depend.

I'll talk first about memorizing the speech, word for word. Typically, that's how people memorize speeches. Later, I'll talk about using your *meaningful memory* to deliver a speech using only *cue words.*

If it's your own speech (if you're not delivering a speech written by a ghostwriter), first, write it out—the whole thing. Then review it for understanding. (If someone has written it for you, start with the review, in the presence of the writer.) Third, decide (1) how much to memorize at one time, (2) when would be the best time for you to do your memorizing, and (3) how you'll reward yourself for success.

How much to memorize at one time depends on several factors: the time you have available to work on your speech, how rapidly in the past you learned materials like these, how long the speech is, and how clear you already are about the information. You can probably come up with other factors unique to yourself.

Regardless, if you repeat the speech over and over, in small pieces and over a period of time rather than all at once, you'll learn more of the speech much more rapidly and with greater accuracy. It's called *spaced repetition*—the method every high school student should learn to use instead of cramming the night before an exam.

Cramming produces short-term memory only. The information sits in the threshold of consciousness overnight—for two or three days, at best—and then most of it gets swallowed by the clutter in your brain, rarely if ever to be retrieved again. As people say, we forget it.

On the other hand, scientific studies demonstrate that spaced repetition produces long-term memory—information that stays in the threshold of consciousness for as long as you continue to repeat the materials.

If, however, time is short, and you lack the luxury of learning the speech in small pieces, you can learn the speech as a whole—but again, more rapidly and with greater accuracy if you space the repetitions over as much time as you have. You'll gain the advantage of learning the speech as a single unit, giving it more coherence and coordination in the process. That coherence and coordination give you a more meaningful experience that helps you deliver the material as a unit in which no one part lacks the strength of any other part.

Of course, the length of the speech determines whether or not you can learn *wholistically* this way. Attacking an extraordinarily long speech as a whole could lead to what is called *cognitive overload*—trying to take in more than the mind can absorb at one time.

Just as enriching your memory demands greater observational skill on your part, memorizing takes greater concentration than usual. That concentration requires an expenditure of energy, and the brain can expend just so much energy at one time before it gives in. Just how much any one brain can absorb before overloading depends on the individual and the amount of exercise that brain usually gets.

As I've said before, exercising the brain is just like exercising a muscle. The more you develop it, the more and the better it performs.

Memorizing a speech requires concentration, which you can enhance by giving yourself the proper atmosphere in which to memorize your speech. Just what works for you will be somewhat unique to you, but in the accompanying sidebar, I've listed a set of guidelines that have been shown to help the brain do its work.

The cue-word outline I described earlier will make memorizing a speech much easier, because you will be memorizing the key components of your material

Enhancing Your Ability to Memorize a Speech

1. Find a relatively quiet place, not a profoundly silent room. You'll probably fall asleep there.

2. Keep the room's temperature moderate—not too hot or too cold. Either extreme will take away from your ability to concentrate.

3. Prevent interruptions. Ask your secretary to hold your calls. Hang a "Do Not Disturb" sign on your door.

4. To prevent yourself from interrupting yourself, take care of all pressing matters you can think of before starting to work. Clear your mind of other matters—whatever they might be.

5. Relax, but not too much. A certain amount of tension helps—sitting on a mildly uncomfortable chair, walking about the room as you recite, feeling a bit of anxiety, a sense of urgency.

6. Avoid chemical substances of all sorts. Contrary to the conventional wisdom, neither drugs nor alcohol improve concentration; in fact, they interfere with it.

7. Schedule your work period around your peak times—times when you tend to feel the best and accomplish the most.

8. Set realistic, achievable goals and objectives. Using the due date of the speech (or whatever the deadline of the task) as the starting place, work backward in your schedule to identify how much you have to accomplish by each milestone in your plan.

9. Reward yourself when you succeed in reaching a milestone. During each work session, work

toward a target and work for some payoff in addition to the goal: a favorite soft drink, a bit of time off—something you'd like to have that you ordinarily wouldn't permit yourself except for a special occasion.

----

rather than memorizing it whole. However, for this approach to work best, the subject matter has to be something with which you're familiar, even if someone else has written the talk.

The cue-word outline works the same way when you learn a speech as when you listen to one. Cue words impact on memory the same way in both cases.

Guideline No. 5 in the sidebar ("walking about the room as you *recite*") explains how come the cue-word outline works the same way whether you're memorizing the whole speech or working off a memorized cue-word outline. Namely, reciting a speech means talking out loud.

Talking out loud and thinking aloud are two sides of the same coin. You hear yourself think, just the way you hear another person think, when you speak out loud. Studies confirm that you retain far more of what you say out loud than what you recite subvocally. When you recite a speech from a cue-word outline, you take full advantage of meaningful memory. Here's how you do it.

Since, when listening to a speech, you jot down only the words you hear emphasized, then when writing a speech, you jot down only the words you intend to emphasize. You can do that in one of two ways.

If you're thoroughly versed in the subject matter of the speech, write only a topic outline. Use 3″ × 5″ cards, one topic per card, and organized in the order that makes the most sense for your talk as a whole. The cards are easier to carry around than a folder of papers.

If you're first learning about the subject—or if you're not accustomed either to writing or to speech making—write out your entire speech from a topic outline. Review the speech several times, reading it aloud each time, getting a feel for the rhythm you want, for the tones you want to convey, and for the unity you want to transmit. Then, use your topic outline for working through each topic until it is fixed firmly in your mind.

The topic outline consists of cue words, each of which embodies a main or primary idea. Everything else either supports these key topics or describes them or explains them or elaborates on them. If you know what you're talking about, learning those cue words gives you the sense, substance, and organization of your talk. From there, the rest is easy.

Whether you've written out the whole speech or you've written only a cue-word outline, recitation takes another important form. As you know, no actor goes on stage without rehearsal. Experienced, well-trained narrators, newscasters, and other *readers* of material need very little rehearsal. But actors? That's another story.

And what is a rehearsal other than reciting your speech in front of other people? O.K. Call it a dry run. Call it a practice session. It makes no difference. Whatever you call it, by doing it and getting feedback in four ways, you'll improve your memory of the speech.

The first piece of feedback you get is hearing yourself make the presentation in front of other people. Even if it's your spouse or your closest friend or your boss—or some group of these people—treat the rehearsal as if it were the real thing. Every rehearsal is a dress rehearsal.

In front of a group, you sound different than when talking to yourself. Your tempo, your cadences, your tone of voice change, and you need to hear yourself under those circumstances. If you can tape that performance, do so.

You might want to rehearse in front of mirror, even though other people are in the room, because your posture, your gestures, your facial expressions change as well. Seeing yourself gesture to emphasize a point helps you remember that point, especially if it's a cue word.

Feedback comes from your audience in two ways also. Watch them as you talk. Watch their body language. Do they seem bored at some point? Do they seem interested or enthusiastic about what you're saying?

The bored expressions help you change the material or the delivery of it and force you to give that particular section extra rehearsal time—thereby reinforcing your memory of it. Now, if bored expressions help reinforce memory, you can imagine what interest or enthusiasm will do.

The final piece of feedback comes from what your audience tells you about your speech—the parts that bored them, the parts that interested them or excited them. Those data help you fine-tune the speech even more. And the more you work on the speech, the easier it will be to recall it when you deliver it.

Chapter 7

Remembering Numbers and Appointments

Now there are nine-digit zip codes, eleven-digit telephone numbers—even longer phone numbers if you need an access code or an international connection. And we thought we had it tough when all we had to learn was our social security numbers.

Let's start with the eleven-digit phone number. Obviously, since the brain has difficulty memorizing a string of numbers, the simplest way to absorb them is to break the long string into shorter units. For example, if you're outside the Dallas area code, to dial Dallas information, you need to know the numbers 12145551212. By setting off the area code in parentheses, you break up the string. If you learn the number as "one, two-fourteen, five-fifty-five, twelve-twelve," you've broken it down even further. For most people, this method works well enough.

But some people like to use a more elaborate, but somewhat difficult, method for remembering long numbers. It's called a "key-word alphabet," and if you like playing with cryptographic puzzles, you'll enjoy using this system, as well.

Words are easier to remember than numbers. They're more meaningful than abstract numbers and nestle neatly into accessible memory.

This method, relying on the principle of association, correlates letters with numbers. You can then substitute words for the numbers you need to memorize.

Once you've gotten words with which to work, you can visualize associations, too.

Take a look at the sidebar entitled "The Key-Word Alphabet." It correlates consonant sounds with the numbers *0* through *9*. It's true, you really have to test your memory to memorize the table, but once you do it, you'll be able to perform amazingly difficult feats of numerical memory.

The Key-Word Alphabet

1	2	3	4	5	6	7	8	9	0
t	*n*	*m*	*r*	*l*	*j*	*k*	*f*	*p*	*s*
d					*sh*	hard *g*	*v*	*b*	*z*
th					*ch*	hard *c*	*ph*		soft *c*
					soft *g*	*ng*			
					tch				
					dg				

You shouldn't have too much trouble with the numbers *2, 3, 4,* and *5.* Each of them is represented by only one consonant sound. And see how the numbers and letters are connected. The letter *n* consists of *two* downstrokes; the letter *m* consists of *three* strokes. The spelling of the number *4* ends with the letter *r;* and the five fingers of the hand, if you extend your thumb outward, form the letter *L.* That's pretty simple.

Connecting the letters with the numbers *1, 6, 7, 8, 9,* and *0*—that takes some practice. While practicing, keep the alphabet in front of you until you develop dexterity with it.

You've probably noticed that this system doesn't use the vowels—*a, e, i, o,* and *u*—or the letters *h, w, x,* and *y*. None of them fits the phonetic sounds of the numbers.

O.K. First, practice in reverse. Here's a sentence. Translate it into numbers. Remember, vowels and *h, w, x,* and *y* don't count. Use only the consonants.

> *The woman is lovely.*

Got it? If you said "1 3 2 0 5 8 5," you did get it.

> *The woman is lovely.*
> 1   3 2 0 5 8 5

Broken down into a list of correlates, the sentence and numbers look like this:

T = *1* (*h* and *e* don't count)
m = *3* (*w, o,* and *a* don't count)
n = *2*
s = *0* (*i* doesn't count)
l = *5* (*o* doesn't count)
v = *8* (*e* doesn't count)
l = *5* (*y* doesn't count)

I started with a sentence first to show you that meaningful sentences will help make memorizing the numbers easier for you than just assigning random letter combinations. You could represent each number by a different word, a word that has a phonetic connection with the number. For example, *toes* = *10*. Check that against the key-word alphabet. Every time you need to remember the number *10,* just think *toes.*

Take any long number and translate it into a sentence—like this:

57278328404109740
Lou, king of men, frees right speakers.

5	=	*Lou*
727	=	*king*
8	=	*of*
32	=	*men*
840	=	*frees*
41	=	*right*
09740	=	*speakers*

Not all long numbers will fit neatly into meaningful sentences. Therefore, it's to your advantage to tie single words to each number—words that you can recall easily (for example, *hut* for *1,* where the *t* is all that counts; *hen* for *2,* where the *n* is all that counts; *hum* for *3; hear* for *4; heel* for *5; huge* for *6; hug* for *7; have* for *8; hub* for *9; has* for *0.* Pick words comfortable for you to remember, but notice that each of mine began with an *h* and had only one consonant.

Now, just for practice, try applying my list to the following number:

08043572196

You should have "has, have, has, hear, hum, heel, hug, hen, hut, hub, huge."

How you set up your key words, based on the key-word alphabet, is strictly up to you. Some people even translate teens and twenties (such as *tot* for *11, nose* for *20*). You choose the words that work best for you, and you develop the number of words with which you're most comfortable. Once you get used to this system, you will be able to remember numbers far better than you ever could before.

Remembering Appointments and Other Dates

A special case of remembering numbers is remembering appointments or other dates, such as birthdays and anniversaries. You have an appointment with Sam Brown on June 10. Your niece's birthday is July 1. How do you keep them straight in your mind?

Obviously, a good date book or calendar (a computer, if you have one) gives you the best memory possible. But if you're like some people, you forget to look at your own notes. Even if you write down the important dates, by using the principle of association, you can fix them in your mind, as well.

Let's take the birthday first. Susan's birthday is July 1. How does that translate, given the key-word alphabet? Let's try, "Susan is a cutie." *Susan* = 7 1.

Leave Susan's name alone. You're trying to remember her birthdate. Translate *is* as *equals* ($=$), then the date $7 = c$, $t = 1$. Vowels (*u*, *i*, and *e*) don't count. Not only will you remember Susan's birthday; she'll love you for thinking she's cute.

Now, Sam Brown may not appreciate being called a cutie. You'd better come up with something else for remembering your appointment with him on June 10. You could come up with a sentence similar to the one you used for your niece's birthday. Or you could assign colors to every day in the week of June 10. Let's say June 10 is on a Tuesday this year. Then, for that week, the days are Maroonday, Brownday, Whiteday, Greenday, Yellowday. June 10 is *Brown*day, the day you meet with Sam Brown. But at what time?

Ten o'clock. The appointment's at 10:00 A.M. How important is that appointment? Is it worth money to you? How much money? At least ten dollars, right?

O.K. Your appointment, then, is with Sam Brown on Brownday, and it's worth $10.00. Brownday is Tuesday, June 10, and $10.00 is 10:00 A.M. In short, make associations that work for you, even if they seem to make little or no immediate sense. Sometimes the absurd lingers in your accessible memory more persistently than the rational.

Conclusion

No one need suffer from absentmindedness or forgetfulness. I'm not saying that by reading this book—or any other—you'll develop an infallible memory. I'm only saying that you can get your memory to work better for you if you'll work hard for it.

This summary section will help you test how well you remember what I said. It's deliberately written vaguely. You might call it a narrative cue-word outline. As you read each paragraph, write, think out loud, or tell someone else what you remember about each topic. If you took notes as you read, you can compare your recollection with them.

The brain's a vast storehouse of anything you've ever experienced, whether you're aware of the experiences or not. You can, however, improve the quality of what you remember by becoming more alert to your own needs and what needs those memories satisfy.

By becoming goal-directed, you guide your memory toward those matters that are most important, immediate, or fruitful for you. You set priorities among the experiences you store in your threshold of consciousness as readily accessible memories. You relegate to deeper, inaccessible recesses of your memory anything that ranks lower in your value system.

By paying attention to the world in which you live, you engage all your senses simultaneously, picking up more and more cues you can use for retrieving a thought, an experience, an idea, an image, a name, a sequence of words or numbers, a face. A regularly active brain performs greater feats of memory than does a sluggish one.

Listening to a speech or memorizing one to deliver both benefit from the use of a cue-word outline, one in which a single word or a short phrase captures the essence of the thought. The cue words act as hooks that catch the rest of the material and bring it into focus.

When memorizing a speech, using repetition helps to *store* the words and their meanings. However, the use of spaced repetition helps *secure* the words and their meanings, whether you're learning the speech wholistically or in parts. Reciting and rehearsing the speech out loud helps *burn* the talk into your memory.

Retaining what you read depends on how you read rather than on how much you read. Of course, the more you read effectively, the more you exercise your brain, and the better your brain performs. Scanning, previewing, and skimming will help you increase both your skill in reading for acquaintance and your skill in reading for in-depth understanding. However, reading for in-depth understanding demands attention, interest, producing a cue-word outline (or at least marginal notes), and review. By working on what you read, you retain it more completely, more accurately, and in a form that is more readily accessible.

Names and faces become easier to remember when you use visualization (or creative imagery) and the principle of association (the laws of similarity, opposites, togetherness, frequency, recency, and vividness) as mnemonic devices. By combining those devices with the key-word alphabet, your memory for numbers will become unbeatable.

Many systems exist that you can use for improving your memory. At the same time, once you understand how these principles of memory enhancement work, you can develop any system that is most effective for you.

Now, if I gave you a pop quiz right this minute, how much detail about this book would you be able to recall?

Index

accessible memory, 4, 5, 22–24, 34, 54
acquaintance reading, 27, 28–29, 30, 33, 54
afterimage, memory, 13, 17
alphabet, key-word, 48–51
appointments, 52–53
association(s), 11, 13
  appointment, 52–53
  defined, 14–17
  name and object, 18, 19
  vocabulary, 24

clutter, 7–8, 28, 35
cognitive overload, 43
consciousness, 4
consensus, 38–39
cramming, 42
cue-word outline, 30–33
  memorization and, 43–47
  in speech retention, 53, 54

dates, 52–53
distractions, 26, 31, 34

emotions, 33, 35–36
eye contact, 36–37

faces, remembering, 18–22

feedback
  paraphrasing and, 35–36
  speeches and, 46–47
frequency law, 16

goal setting, 3, 9–10, 53
  reading and, 31
  see also priorities

inaccessible memory, 4, 5, 54
in-depth reading, 27, 29–30, 33, 54

key-word alphabet, 48–51

law(s) of:
  frequency, 16
  opposites, 16, 18
  recency, 16
  similarity, 15, 18, 19
  togetherness, 16, 18
  vividness, 16–17, 18
listening, 19–20, 33
  participative, 33, 34–39

meaningful memory, 6
  listening and, 34
  priorities and, 8–9
  scanning and, 28
  speeches and, 41–42

memorization, 29
  of speeches, 42–47
  word power and, 23–24
memory
  accessible, 4, 5, 22–24, 34, 54
  afterimage, 13, 17
  inaccessible, 4, 5, 54
  meaningful, 6, 8–9, 28, 34, 41–42
  short-term, 23, 42
mnemonic devices, 13, 15

names, remembering, 18–22
note-taking, 31–33
numbers, remembering, 48–51

objects, remembering, 18–22
observation, 11–13
  listening and, 34, 36–37
  reading and, 31
  use of, 18, 19–20
opposites law, 16, 18
overload, cognitive, 43

paraphrasing, 31–33, 35–36
previewing, 28, 29, 30, 31
principle, of association, 54–55
priorities
  criteria for, 7
  importance of, 8–9, 53
  reading, 28, 30
  see also goal-setting

questions, for clarification, 37

reading
  for acquaintance, 27, 28–29, 30, 33
  cue-word outlines for, 30–33
  flaws in, 26–27

in-depth, 27, 29–30, 33
  vocabulary and, 25–26
recall
  memorization and, 22–24
  visualization and, 14
  see also retrieval, information
recency law, 16
regression, 26–27
repetition
  frequency and, 16
  short-term memory and, 23
  spaced, 42–43, 54
retrieval, information, 2, 4, 22
  see also recall
review, 27, 30–33

scanning, 28–29, 30, 31
short-term memory, 23, 42
similarity law, 15, 18, 19
skimming, 28, 29, 30, 31
sound-alikes, 15
spaced repetition, 42–43, 54
speeches
  cue-word outlines for, 39–41, 43–47
  memorization of, 42–47
storage, information, 2, 4, 6
subvocalizing, 26, 45
suppression, 5

togetherness law, 16, 18

visualization, 11, 13
  afterimage and, 13–14
  name and face, 18, 19, 54
vividness, 36
  law of, 16–17, 18
vocabulary power
  cue-word outline for, 39–40
  development of, 22–24
  reading for, 25
vocalizing, 26, 45

About the Author

Donald H. Weiss is an Account Executive for Psychological Associates, a training and development company, and President of Self-Management Associates, a small-business consulting firm located in Dallas. Along with the six books in the Successful Office Skills series, he has written numerous books, articles, video scripts, and study guides on business management and related topics. Dr. Weiss is also the author of AMACOM's popular cassette/workbook programs *Getting Results, How to Manage for Higher Productivity,* and *Managing Conflict.*

Dr. Weiss holds a Ph.D. in social theory from Tulane University, as well as degrees from the University of Arizona and the University of Missouri. He has also taught at several colleges and universities. He is a member of the American Society for Training and Development.